MILITARY MACHINES

HELICOPTERS

QEB Publishing

Editor: Lauren Taylor
Designer: Izzy Langridge
Educational consultant: Jillian Harker

Copyright © QEB Publishing, Inc. 2012

First published in the United States
by QEB Publishing, Inc
3 Wrigley Suite A
Irvine, CA 92618

www.qed-publishing.co.uk

ISBN 978 1 60992 291 7

Printed in China

A CIP record for this title is available from the Library of Congress..

Picture Credits:
army.mil 16-17 Kelly Patrice Pate, 22-23
Mass Communication Specialist 2nd
Class Matthew A. Ebarb
Corbis 10-11 George Hall, 12-13 U.S.
Navy, 18-19 Antonio Bat/epa
defenceimages.mod.uk 8R SAC Andy
Stevens – Crown Copyright
Getty 20-21 Frank Rossoto Stocktrek
Shutterstock 1 Arie v.d. Wolde, 2 David
Acosta Allely, 7-8 Peter R Foster IDMA,
14-15 Thor Jorgen Udvang, 24 Elenamiv
U.S. Air Force Photo FC Senior Airman
Noah R. Johnson, 4-5 Senior Airman
Brian Ferguson, 6-7 Airman 1st Class
Jessica Green

Words in **bold** appear in
the glossary on page 24

CONTENTS

What Is a Helicopter?

A helicopter is a type of **aircraft**. Helicopters are very useful because they don't need a **runway**. They can land almost anywhere. All around the world, **armies** and **navies** fly helicopters.

Armies and navies move people and equipment, and rescue people with helicopters. They also fight enemy tanks with helicopters.

How Do Helicopters Fly?

The long, thin blades on top of a helicopter are called the **rotor**. Each blade works like a wing. When the rotor spins very fast, the rotors lift the helicopter into the air.

rotor

The rotor also makes the helicopter fly forward, backward, and sideways. The rotor is turned by an **engine**.

Flying a Helicopter

The **cockpit** is at the front of a helicopter. The pilot sits in here. He or she pushes and pulls on handles and pedals that control the rotor and other parts of the helicopter.

Pilots often have to fly very fast and very close to the ground. This takes skill and a lot of training.

pilot in cockpit

Takeoff and Landing

To take off, a helicopter
pilot uses more engine power to
make the rotor spin fast. The helicopter
lifts slowly into the air. The pilot pushes
a handle to make the helicopter
move forward.

To land, the pilot makes the
helicopter slow down. Then he or she
cuts the engine power down to let the
helicopter drop slowly to the ground.

Attack Helicopters

An attack helicopter is a helicopter that fights enemy tanks and shoots at other equipment. The pilot flies fast and close to the ground. This makes it hard for enemy fighters to see the helicopter.

The helicopter fires guns and **missiles**.
An attack helicopter has thick metal
plates called **armor** to stop
enemy bullets from harming it.

Apache

The Apache is an attack helicopter.
The US Army and the British Army
both fly Apache helicopters to
fight enemy tanks.

FACTS

Length	57.7 feet (17.6 meters)
Rotor size	47.9 feet (14.6 meters)
Height	16 feet (4.9 meters)
Top speed	205mph (330kph)
Weight	4.8 tons (7.7 tonnes)
Capacity	2 soldiers
Crew	2
Weapons	Missiles, rockets, and a cannon

Transport Helicopters

Transport helicopters have a big space inside called a hold. They carry soldiers and things the soldiers need, such as food, rockets, and bullets.

Large transport helicopters can carry heavy vehicles or big guns. The vehicle or gun dangles underneath the helicopter on chains.

Chinook

The Chinook is a giant transport helicopter with two big rotors. It has a ramp at the back to load **cargo** into its cargo hold.

FACTS

Length	98.7 feet (30.1 meters)
Rotor size	60 feet (18.3 meters)
Height	18.7 feet (5.7 meters)
Top speed	195mph (315kph)
Weight	13.3 tons (12.1 tonnes)
Capacity	55 soldiers or 13.2 tons (12 tonnes) of cargo
Crew	3
Weapons	Machine guns

Rescue Helicopters

Rescue helicopters carry soldiers who are hurt from a battle to a hospital. Helicopters that carry hurt soldiers have red crosses painted on them.

Military helicopters often help after disasters such as earthquakes and floods. They rescue trapped people and deliver food and medicine.

Helicopters at Sea

Many large navy ships have their own helicopters. The helicopters hunt for enemy ships and carry stores. Landing a helicopter on the deck of a ship is very hard, even in calm weather.

Search and rescue helicopters also help find people lost at sea, and rescue people from sinking boats and ships.

GLOSSARY

aircraft
A machine made for flying through the air

armor
A metal covering to protect against harm

army
A large number of people ready and trained for warfare

cargo
A load carried by a ship, aircraft, or other vehicle

cockpit
The space in an aircraft for the pilot and crew

engine
A machine that can use energy to power something

missile
A flying bomb used to attack an enemy

navy
A group of people who use warships and other equipment to fight at sea

rotor
The long, thin blades on top of a helicopter

runway
A hard, wide surface from which aircraft take off and on which they land